JESUS LOVES CHILDREN

A Bible story, "Jesus Blessing the Little Children," based on Matthew 19, Mark 10, Luke 18

Lynn Groth

Copyright 1985 by the Board for Parish Education
Wisconsin Ev. Lutheran Synod
Milwaukee, Wisconsin 53222
All rights reserved. Printed in U.S.A.

ISBN 0-938272-78-0

While Jesus lived upon the earth,
He traveled here and there.
He spoke with people young and old.
He had good news to share.

This work kept Jesus busy,
But He took time to show
His love to little children.
He cares for them, you know!

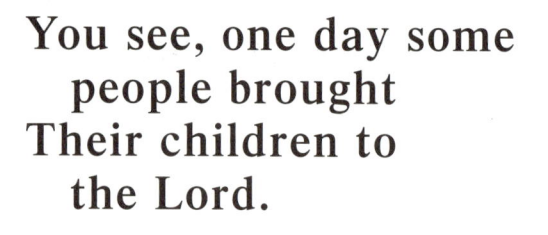

You see, one day some
 people brought
Their children to
 the Lord.

They wanted Him to touch them all
And bless them with His Word.

He told the parents,
   "Come to Me.
Your children bring along.

For children, too, can trust in Me.
They give Me all their love.
Whoever has a faith like theirs
Will live in heaven above."

Then Jesus took them in His arms
And blessed them, one by one.

He loved them with a perfect love,
For He is God's own Son!

(Parents: Make the face resemble your child.)

There is a little face above.
Why, it looks just like you!
How happy you must feel inside,
For Jesus loves you, too!